INDIAN PRAIRIE PUBLIC LIBRARY DISTRICT

3 1946 00222 9711

JAN 5 2000

4-5-09 (17)
5-15-10 (18)
6-15 (19)

Early Ford V-8s
1932 - 1942

D0939914

Photo Album

By James H. Moloney

Iconografix
Photo Album Series

INDIAN PRAIRIE PUBLIC LIBRARY
401 PLAINFIELD ROAD
DARIEN, IL 60561

Iconografix Inc. exists to preserve history through the publication of notable photographic archives and the list of titles under the Iconografix imprint is constantly growing. Transportation enthusiasts should be on the Iconografix mailing list and are invited to write and ask for a catalog, free of charge.

Authors and editors in the field of transportation history are invited to contact the Editorial Department at Iconografix, Inc., PO Box 446, Hudson, WI 54016. We require a minimum of 120 photographs per subject. We prefer subjects narrow in focus, e.g., a specific model, railroad, or racing venue. Photographs must be of high-quality, suited to large format reproduction.

Iconografix
PO Box 446
Hudson, Wisconsin 54016 USA

© 1999 by James H. Moloney

All rights reserved. No part of this work may be reproduced or used in any form by any means... graphic, electronic, or mechanical, including photocopying, recording, taping, or any other information storage and retrieval system... without written permission of the publisher.

The information in this book is true and complete to the best of our knowledge. All recommendations are made without any guarantee on the part of the author or Publisher, who also disclaim any liability incurred in connection with the use of this data or specific details.

We acknowledge that certain words, such as model names and designations, mentioned herein are the property of the trademark holder. We use them for purposes of identification only. This is not an official publication.

Iconografix books are offered at a discount when sold in quantity for promotional use. Businesses or organizations seeking details should write to the Marketing Department, Iconografix, at the above address.

Library of Congress Card Number: 98-75274

ISBN 1-882256-97-2

99 00 01 02 03 04 05 5 4 3 2 1

Printed in the United States of America

Cover and book design by Shawn Glidden

Collectors have named the 1932 Ford Roadster as one of the most desirable Fords to own.

INTRODUCTION

In the spring of 1998, I was honored by a call from Rick Seymour, President of Iconografix, asking if I wanted to compile a photo archive book on the early Ford V-8s. Naturally I said yes because I enjoy anything to do with older cars. I never owned an early Ford but have always enjoyed the sound of their peppy engines—especially when they start in low gear and go into second.

For me, the era of the Ford V-8 has always been special because it began a few months after I was born in October, 1931. Of course, I don't recall the 1930s from day one, but my first recollection of Fords was a trip to San Diego, California, in 1935 when we visited a Ford display at a California fair. The various displays showed all of the 1935 Fords in different body styles. The big thing for me was receiving a rubber 1935 Tudor Sedan that a factory representative gave to my dad. I loved it and, believe it or not, I still have it—only a little worse for wear—64 years later.

Many enthusiasts have certain years of the V-8's 11-year span that are more appealing than others. Although I am not the complete authority on design and beauty, I personally like the 1932, 1933, 1934, 1936, and 1940 models the best.

In 1931, the Depression was beginning to slow down Ford sales and Ford needed to do something, and fast, to stay in the automobile market. The Model-A couldn't continue, as had the Model-T, for a run of 15 years or

longer. So with a brainchild in the works, the V-8 thought was born, and by the spring of 1932, the V-8 was seen along with the Model B (4-cylinder cars) in dealerships throughout the country. The public liked them and Ford had another long-term winner in its pocket.

The models that followed had appeal to all. I don't think I've ever heard a person say they didn't like the 1933 or 1934 cars. The only comment I've ever heard is that it sure is hard to tell the difference, at a quick glance, between the two years. I think we all agree. By the middle of 1934, the Model B engine unit was discontinued.

The 1935 and 1936 cars had their own following, too. A brand-new body style appeared in 1935 and took the company on a two-year run that most manufacturers were now doing. For the first time in 25 years, Ford introduced its cars at the New York Auto Show on December 27, 1934. To represent its various body styles, the Ford display occupied three floors of the show. The new cars reflected a heavier, more spacious, and rounded body style, giving them a look of up-to-the-minute styling. The 1936 cars were just more rounded than the predecessor of 1935. Both front and rear fenders were redesigned; the grille was wider and carried vertical bars set in stainless steel, giving a look of real class.

Beginning with the 1937 model year, cars again saw an entirely new design—many people felt it resembled a baby Zephyr. The V-8 engine saw so many improvements that it could almost have been classed as a brand-new engine. The headlamp treatment was now molded into the catwalks, rather than standing on their own perches. A brand-new V-shaped windshield was one of the big pluses in 1937 cars.

In 1938, the two distinct body styles—the Standard and the DeLuxe—were easy for people to distinguish between. The sheet metal for each series was entirely different. Possibly, the thinking was to have the Standard as a low-priced car and the DeLuxe a slightly higher-priced car—the mid-price offering, the Mercury, would be offered the next year. At any rate, it's anybody's guess.

In 1939, Ford's big news—which should have happened long before—was the introduction of hydraulic brakes. Besides this, new sheet metal was seen for the DeLuxe cars and there was a general freshening up for Standard models. But the biggest news from the Ford Motor Company was the unveiling of its new Mercury, which kind of put Ford in the shadow for 1939. The arrival of the 1940 Fords included a great facelift on the DeLuxe models, which were already nice-looking

cars. New for the season was a column shift lever and sealed beam headlamps. The Standard models didn't receive as much of a change from the previous year, but enough to let you know it was a brand-new car.

In 1941, a brand-new body design appeared and a totally new engine was seen under the hood. Each of the models—Special, Standard, and Super DeLuxe—resembled each other more than previous cars did. This "square box" design would be Ford's styling until the new post-war bodies of 1949 appeared.

The 1942 cars were produced for a short-lived season—coming on the market in the fall of 1941 and ending February 10, 1942, due to World War II. Any vehicles built from January 1, 1942, to February 10, 1942, were referred to as "blackout" models, due to the absence of chrome, except for the bumpers. Figures vary as to how many 1942 Fords were produced, but most figures agree it was under 138,500 vehicles.

Well, folks, I hope you enjoy browsing through this photo album and maybe seeing your favorite body style—better yet, you might see your exact car!

Regards,
Jim Moloney
September 1998

A 1932 Ford Roadster with its top in the up position. A total of 6,893 were built as V-8s and 3,719 were equipped with a 4-cylinder engine.

A racy-looking Roadster with both its top and windshield in the down position. This 1932 model delivered for $500 as a V-8, and $50 less if a four was under the hood.

The 1932 Ford Standard Coupe with body by Murray. A total of 28,904 came as V-8s and 20,342 delivered with the 4-cylinder engine.

Heavyweight boxing champion Jack Dempsey sits proudly behind the wheel of the 1932 DeLuxe Coupe. The body is by Murray.

The 1932 Sport Coupe sold for $535 in V-8 fashion and $485 with the Model B engine employed. It was the only model that used the landau irons.

A 1932 Cabriolet available only in DeLuxe trim. The body was by Briggs. A total run of 5,926 units were produced between the 4-cylinder and V-8 configurations.

Ford's first V-8 engine as displayed in 1932.

The 1932 Tudor Ford in DeLuxe style. The unit sold for $500 and was the most popular body style for 1932. A total of 117,396 units were produced for the year.

The 1932 Ford Victoria with body by Murray. This Tudor didn't sell as well as the regular Tudor Sedan but is more collectible today. It was available only in DeLuxe trim.

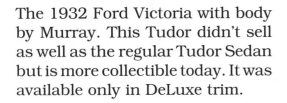

A 1932 DeLuxe Fordor Sedan with body by Briggs. As a V-8, it delivered for $645. A total of 21,500 units sold in V-8 and 4-cylinder fashion.

The 1932 Ford Convertible Sedan with the top in the down position. Only 842 were delivered with the V-8 engine and, worse yet, only 42 saw daylight with a 4-cylinder engine being employed.

With its top in the up position, this Convertible Sedan delivered for $600. 1932 was the final year for this version of the Convertible Sedan, which was virtually a carryover from the Model A.

A 1932 Ford DeLuxe Phaeton with body by Briggs. A total of 2,280 units were manufactured between 4-cylinder and V-8 models.

The 1932 DeLuxe Phaeton with top and windshield in the down position. The car sold for $545 as a V-8 and $50 less with the four employed.

Rare when new and equally hard to locate today is the 1932 Sedan Delivery by LeBaron. Only 402 were produced. Basically, it was a Tudor Sedan with the rear windows enclosed and a door installed in the rear panel.

A late-season offering for 1932 was this open-cab Pickup with body by Briggs—the unit did not appear until May. The top was non-collapsible. It came only as a 4-cylinder with a production run of 593 units.

The 1932 Ford Station Wagon, with body by Baker-Rawling, drew 351 customers for the V-8 engine; 1,032 preferred it as a 4-cylinder. Prices were $600 as a four and $650 for the V-8.

Ford's 1932 DeLuxe Panel body by Budd carried the designation of Type B-79. It came with all of the front-end passenger-car components. Most of the production carried the 4-cylinder engine.

The lowest-priced Ford Coupe for 1933 was the five-window Coupe with body by Murray. Most came with the V-8 engine. Only 23 examples employed the 4-cylinder version.

A fashionable three-window 1933 Coupe, body by Murray, sold for $540 when the V-8 engine was used. The rumble seat was an extra cost option.

The 1933 Victoria was an entirely new style for the year; it was referred to as Type 740. The body was built by Murray. A total of 4,218 were produced.

Not seen too often is this 1933 side-mounted and rear-mounted spare example. The Tudor model, as with all 1933 and 1934 cars, was referred to as Model 40.

A 1933 DeLuxe Tudor Sedan with body by Briggs. The Tudor again was Ford's most popular model for the year, with a total production of 109,298 units.

Next to the Station Wagon this 1933 DeLuxe Fordor Sedan was the company's most expensive car, selling for $610. It weighed 2,684 pounds.

Here it is, Ford's most expensive vehicle for 1933: the Station Wagon, Type 860, selling for $640. The body builder was Murray.

A 1933 Roadster by Murray. Removable side curtains took the place of roll-up side windows. Note the flap in the side curtain, making arm signals more accessible.

The top down on this 1933 Roadster makes for a day of fresh air. Note the accessory hood ornament that adorns this vehicle.

An easy telltale feature between 1933 and 1934 Fords is seen in this photo. The 1933 had only one hood latch, while 1934s carried two handles.

The 1933 Cabriolet with body by Murray. A production run of 7,852 V-8s were produced; only 24 4-cylinders were delivered.

A 1933 DeLuxe Phaeton, body by Murray. A total of only 2,413 units, both in Standard and DeLuxe styles, were produced for 1933.

A snappy looking unit is this 1933 Sedan Delivery, Type 850. As a V-8, it delivered for $570 and, if the 4-cylinder were employed, the price was $520. It was built by LeBaron, a division of Briggs Manufacturing Company.

INDIAN PRAIRIE PUBLIC LIBRARY
401 PLAINFIELD ROAD
DARIEN, IL 60561

The 1934 Ford Victoria with body by Murray. A total production of 20,083 was produced— all used the V-8 power plant. The car sold for $610.

This 1934 unit differed from the 1933 Victoria by having a swing-out trunk panel that became available in May of that year.

A 1934 Ford with the built-in accessory trunk on display at Meier-Frank Ford Dealership.

Edsel and Henry Ford, with a company executive, stand proudly beside the one millionth Ford: a 1934 Fordor Sedan.

The 1934 Ford DeLuxe Phaeton with body by Murray. Ford produced 1,413 of this model in 4-cylinder and V-8 form, coming in Standard and DeLuxe trim.

The attractive 1934 Roadster sits with its top down; it sold for $525 as a V-8. A total of 5,070 DeLuxe Roadsters were built for the year. All but 32 were equipped with the V-8 power plant.

This 1934 Ford Cabriolet came only in DeLuxe trim. The vehicle sold for $590 with a production run of 14,496. Only 12 customers ordered the 4-cylinder version.

A DeLuxe 3-window Coupe for 1934. A total of 22,692 in Standard and Deluxe styles were manufactured for the year. The vehicle was available for $555.

A five-window 1934 Coupe equipped with the accessory 14-inch wheels and McGlaren Air-Ride Tires. Note the accessory Greyhound hood ornament, too.

As the Gerber door indicates, this five-window 1934 Coupe was for fleet use. Ford sold 45,217 of this body style for the year in both 4-cylinder and V-8. The 4-cylinder was discontinued in May of that year.

A sad day for someone, this once sharp 1934 Roadster crashed.

Ford's most expensive car for 1934 was this Station Wagon, Type 860. It sold for $660. The production run was 3,000 units with only 95 using the 4-cylinder power plant.

This 1934 Sedan Delivery mostly used components from the passenger car line. The body was by Briggs with a production run of 9,811 units. Of that total, only 483 came with the 4-cylinder engine.

Ford offered a new body style beginning with the 1935 cars and lasting for a two-year run. Seen here is the DeLuxe Fordor Slantback Sedan, which had a production run of 124,983 units. The car sold for $655.

The 1935 Ford Fordor Touring Sedan with body by Briggs. A total of 105,157 of this model found buyers in the model run.

The 1935 Tudor Touring Sedan with body by Briggs was only available in DeLuxe trim. It was designated Type 700 and sold for the same price as the Slantback Tudor—$595.

A well-dressed 1935 DeLuxe Tudor Sedan with accessory wheel covers and the winterfront over the grille. This example went out the door for $595 to 84,692 customers.

The most expensive and lowest production went to this model, the 1935 Convertible Sedan, Type 740. It sold for $750 and had a run of 4,234 units produced.

The 1935 Ford Phaeton, with body by Murray, delivered for $580 and carried a production run of 6,073 orders.

The 1935 Phaeton came only in DeLuxe trim with its interior done in gray-brown genuine leather. The windwings, as shown here, were standard equipment.

The 1935 Phaeton with its top down. This was Ford's final year to use wire wheels.

Ford's five-window Coupe with body by Murray. A total of 33,065 were delivered in this DeLuxe style. Another 45,412 came as Standard Coupes, giving a total of 78,477 five-window Coupes produced in 1935.

A little more sporty looking than the five-window Coupe is this 1935 three-window Coupe, which had a run of 31,513 sold. The Murray bodied Coupe delivered for $570.

This 1935 Roadster, Type 710, was only available in DeLuxe form with rumble seat. The unit weighed 2,597 pounds and delivered for $550.

The 1935 Cabriolet also came only in DeLuxe trim, with a more expensive price than the Roadster. It sold for $625. A total of 17,000 were built.

A display of 1935 Fords shown at a Belgian auto show.

The 1935 Ford Station Wagon, body by Murray, was the second most expensive Ford produced that year. It delivered for $670. A total of 4,536 were produced.

Ford's 1935 Sedan Delivery, Type 780, delivered for $585 to 8,308 customers. It carried a body by Briggs, using the front-end passenger-car components.

A series of 1935 Fords comes down the assembly line. In the foreground is the Tudor DeLuxe Sedan.

In May 1936, this Ford DeLuxe Fordor Sedan was the three millionth V-8 produced. Note the extra cost spider wheel covers.

The DeLuxe Fordor Touring Sedan for 1936. This vehicle cost $650 and was one of 159,825 produced, which also included the Standard model.

The 1936 DeLuxe Fordor Sedan with body by Briggs was often referred to as the Slantback Sedan. It was never as popular as the Trunkback version, however. A total of 74,372 Slantbacks were produced for the year, which also includes the Standard version.

A 1936 DeLuxe Tudor Touring Sedan selling for $590. A total of 125,303 DeLuxe examples were sold for the year.

To me, one of the sharpest Ford's ever built was this three-window 1936 Coupe with body by Murray. It sold for $570 to 21,446 customers.

A 1936 DeLuxe five-window Coupe with body by Murray delivered for $555. A rumble seat option was available for $25 extra. A total of only 29,938 found customers.

The 1936 Cabriolet with a Murray body saw a production of 14,068 units and sold for $625.

The 1936 DeLuxe Roadster saw fewer customers than the Cabriolet—only 3,882 found homes. The vehicle delivered for $560.

New for the season was the Club Cabriolet, which didn't make its debut until March 1936. This example set the tone for future convertibles from Ford.

Another new body style added for the year was the Bustle-Back Convertible Touring Sedan. It was Ford's most expensive offering for 1936, delivering for $780.

Available from April 1936 to the end of the model run was this Trunkback Convertible Sedan. A total of 5,601 were built, which also included the Slantback style.

The 1936 Ford Convertible Sedan differed from the Phaeton in that it offered roll-up windows and the top, when raised, made for a weather-tight interior. It sold for $20 less than the Trunkback version.

The 1936 Phaeton was one of the poorer sellers in the Ford line for that year. Today, it is one of the most sought-after models on the market. A total of 5,555 were produced, retailing for $590.

With the side curtains in place, this 1936 Phaeton was ready for inclement weather. The model came only in DeLuxe form and used genuine brown leather for its interior.

Fords on display at a 1936 auto exhibition. Note that most all of these Fords are equipped with the new accessory spider wheel covers and whitewall tires.

All of it comes together at the right time, as seen in the Dearborn, Michigan, assembly plant.

A 1936 Ford Pickup with body by Budd. A total of 69,733 units were produced for the year. Of these, only 2,570 carried DeLuxe trim.

A pair of 1936 Sedan Delivery units, which had a production run of 7,801. Of these, only 209 came with the DeLuxe trim.

Ford's 1937 DeLuxe Coupe saw 26,738 units produced with a base price of $660. The main differences between this model and the Standard were the bright grillwork, the windshield frame, and a plusher interior for DeLuxe cars.

A Standard 1937 Tudor Sedan saw a production run of 308,446. In DeLuxe style, 33,683 found homes. The difference between the two series was in the trim.

The 1937 DeLuxe Tudor Touring drew a $700 price tag for the 69,902 produced.

The most popular four-door model for 1937 was the DeLuxe Fordor Touring, with a production run of 98,687 units sold at a price of $760.

What a few accessories can do to the same Fordor Touring. 1937 was the first year Ford offered fender skirts for its cars. The wheel covers and whitewalls help give it the final touch.

The 1937 Phaeton was not as popular a car as the Convertible Sedan, bringing only 3,723 buyers. It was designated as Type 78-750 and sold for $750.

More popular with the public than the Phaeton was this Convertible Sedan, Type 78-740. A total of 4,378 were sold, all in DeLuxe trim. It was the most expensive Ford for 1937, selling for $860.

The Cabriolet for 1937 was priced at $720. With its roll-up windows, it drew more customers than the Roadster version. A total of 10,148 orders were received.

In 1937, the least popular model was the Roadster, seeing only 1,250 produced. The Murray-built vehicle appeared identical to the Cabriolet, except that it didn't have roll-up windows. This would be the last year for the Roadster.

Gaining in popularity was this 1937 Club Cabriolet with body by Murray. The vehicle, known as Type 760-A, had a production run of 8,001 and delivered for $760.

New for 1937 was the Club Coupe, which found 16,992 customers. The unit delivered for $720. It was known as Type 720.

The 1937 Ford Station Wagon, with body by Murray, found 9,304 buyers. Designated Type 78-790, it sold for $755.

A 1937 Ford Sedan Delivery, available with either the 60 or 85 horsepower engine. A total of 8,548 units were delivered. The base price was $585 with an additional $10 if the 85 horsepower engine was ordered.

A thrifty-looking unit, as it was advertised, the 1937 Pickup with body by Budd. A total of 79,884 units were sold. It was available with either a 60 or 85 horsepower engine.

A 1938 Ford DeLuxe Fordor, which delivered for $770. Due to production difficulties, the Tudor and Fordor Sedans had bodies produced by Briggs, Budd, and Murray. A total of 92,020 were built for the year.

The most popular model in the 1938 DeLuxe line was this Tudor Sedan, which delivered 101,647 units. The vehicle retailed for $725.

This 1938 DeLuxe Club Coupe with body by Murray sold for $745. Sales were not as promising as Ford would have liked, however. Only 7,171 units were delivered. This model was not available in Standard trim.

The 1938 DeLuxe Convertible Club Coupe, with body by Murray, came as a five-passenger model that delivered for $800. It was technically referred to as Type 81A-760B. A total of 6,080 were produced.

A 1938 DeLuxe Convertible Sedan with a Murray body delivered for $900, making it the most expensive model for the year. It outsold the Phaeton, which was discontinued at the end of the model run. A total of 2,743 Convertible Sedans were built in 1938.

For 1938, the Station Wagon came with a new body and side panel bracing, which also included sliding glass in the rear doors and quarter windows. A total of 6,944 units, selling for $825, were delivered. The body was by Iron Mountain, a division of Ford Motor Company.

A series of 1938 Fords shown at one of the Ford shows that were always popular during the Depression years.

An interior shot of the 1938 DeLuxe
Fordor Sedan.

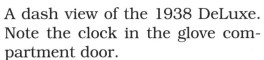

A dash view of the 1938 DeLuxe.
Note the clock in the glove com-
partment door.

The 1939 Standard five-window Coupe, with body by Murray and late year editions, was built by Ford. This was Ford's lowest-priced vehicle, selling for $640 to 38,197 customers.

The second-best seller in the Ford line was this 1939 Standard Tudor Sedan, selling for $680 with a production run of 124,866 units delivered. Customers still had their choice of either the 60 or 85 horsepower engine.

This 1939 DeLuxe Fordor had a production run of 99,377 built, selling for $790.

A popular model in 1939 and today is this DeLuxe five-window Coupe, with body by Murray. A total of 33,326 were delivered with a price tag of $700.

The 1939 Convertible Coupe, Type 76, was the last year for the rumble seat. The year saw 10,422 units assembled with a price of $790.

1939 was the last year for the Convertible Sedan, Type 74, with body by Murray. A total of 3,561 units were sold. The vehicle delivered for $920, making it and the Station Wagon the most expensive Fords for the year.

A total of 6,155 DeLuxe Station Wagons were produced in 1939. The body was by Iron Mountain. Like the Convertible Sedan and Station Wagon, it vied for the most expensive Ford for the year at $920.

A front view of the 1939 DeLuxe wearing some of the Ford factory-approved accessories including roof-mounted antenna, side mirror, and fog lamp.

Ford's International Goodwill Tour advertises the 28 millionth Ford automobile produced. The event took place at the Edgewater, New Jersey, assembly plant on April 8, 1940. Note the license plates mounted on the car hood that represent the states this vehicle had traveled through.

A prototype of the 1940 DeLuxe Fordor Sedan. The vehicle appears with a different style rear hubcap, top-mounted windshield wipers, no front door vent panes, and a different style Ford nameplate affixed to the hood. A total of 91,758 cars were produced in this body style.

The famous aviator Douglas "Wrong Way" Corrigan poses beside his new 1940 Tudor Standard Sedan at the Long Beach, California, assembly plant on August 8, 1940. A total of 150,933 of this model were produced.

Ford's best seller for 1940 was this Tudor DeLuxe Sedan, which drew 171,368 purchasers. It delivered for $765.

What a sad thing to have happened to a sharp-looking car. From the looks of the California license plate, this incident occurred to this 1940 DeLuxe Coupe in 1947.

Always a favorite with me—and most other car enthusiasts—is this beautiful 1940 Ford DeLuxe Coupe. It was available as a business coupe and a five-window Coupe, which actually was a version with two small opera seats behind the front seats. A total of 48,102 of both styles sold for the year. This example wears the Ford script tires.

The 1940 Ford DeLuxe Convertible Coupe, with body by Lincoln, saw a production run of 23,704 units. The car delivered for $850.

With its top in the up position, the 1940 DeLuxe Convertible featured a seating capacity for five passengers. New for the season was a vacuum-operated unit to operate the automatic top.

I love the setting for this 1940 DeLuxe Station Wagon, wearing all of its 1940 Ford accessories. The unit sold for $950, making it the most expensive Ford car for 1940. A total of 8,730 units came on the DeLuxe chassis.

Factory-approved accessories to help dress up the 1940 Ford.

Ford's 1941 DeLuxe Tudor, Type 70-A, had a run of 177,018 units sold. The model delivered for $775.

A 1941 DeLuxe Station Wagon, Type 79-A, sold for $965 and had a production run of 6,116 units. The wagon lacked special body trim, as seen on the Super DeLuxe Wagons.

Ford gave a new title to its top-of-the-line models for 1941. They no longer were called DeLuxe, but were now Super DeLuxe models. This example was the Super DeLuxe coming as a three-passenger and a five-passenger model. The three-passenger sold for $775, while the five-passenger was $25 more.

The 1941 Super DeLuxe Tudor Sedan was Ford's best seller for the year with 185,788 cars sold. It delivered for $820.

Ford now referred to this new body style as the Super DeLuxe Sedan Coupe, Type 72. A total of 45,977 were sold in 1941 for $850.

An early production 1941 Super DeLuxe Fordor Sedan, minus the fender stainless trim, sold for $860. A total of 88,053 were built for the year. Note the deluxe wheel treatment this car received, and its accessory grille guard.

The 1941 Super DeLuxe Convertible Coupe, with body by Lincoln, drew 30,240 customers for $960. Note that this example wears the stainless trim moldings on its fenders that became standard equipment on all Super DeLuxe cars built after January 1, 1941.

This 1941 Super DeLuxe Station Wagon, with body by Iron Mountain, saw 9,485 units delivered for $1,015. This price set the record as being the most expensive Ford built to date.

A 1941 Ford parts room displays its factory-approved parts and accessories.

The 1942 Ford Super DeLuxe Sedan Coupe with body by Ford. It was Type 72-B, priced at $910. A total of only 13,543 were built before production ceased for World War II.

This 1942 Super DeLuxe Fordor Sedan shows a nicely redesigned front-end treatment. A total of 24,846 units were produced in the short model run. The car delivered for $920.

Going up in price again, the 1942 Super DeLuxe Station Wagon, Type 79-B, now sold for $1,100. A total of 5,483 were produced for the short production season.

The grille of the 1942 models was made of pressed steel rather than cast, again to help conserve certain metals for the war effort. This example is displayed with factory approved fog lamps and the swan-style side mirror.

More Titles from Iconografix:

*This product is sold under license from Mack Trucks, Inc. Mack is a registered Trademark of Mack Trucks, Inc. All rights reserved.

All Iconografix books are available from direct mail specialty book dealers and bookstores worldwide, or can be ordered from the publisher. For book trade and distribution information or to add your name to our mailing list contact

Iconografix
PO Box 446
Hudson, Wisconsin, 54016

Telephone: (715) 381-9755
(800) 289-3504 (USA)
Fax: (715) 381-9756

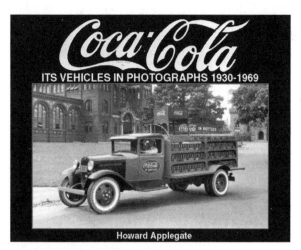

Coca-Cola
ITS VEHICLES IN PHOTOGRAPHS 1930-1969

Howard Applegate

MORE GREAT BOOKS FROM ICONOGRAFIX

COCA-COLA: ITS VEHICLES IN PHOTOGRAPHS 1930-1969
ISBN 1-882256-47-6

COCA-COLA: A HISTORY IN PHOTOGRAPHS 1930-1969
ISBN 1-882256-46/8

AMERICAN SERVICE STATIONS 1935-1943 *Photo Archive*
ISBN 1-882256-27-1

PHILLIPS 66 1945-1954 *Photo Archive* ISBN 1-882256-42-5

LINCOLN MOTOR CARS 1920-1942 *Photo Archive* ISBN 1-882256-57-3

PACKARD MOTOR CARS 1935-1942 *Photo Archive* ISBN 1-882256-44-1

STUDEBAKER 1933-1942 *Photo Archive* ISBN 1-882256-24-7

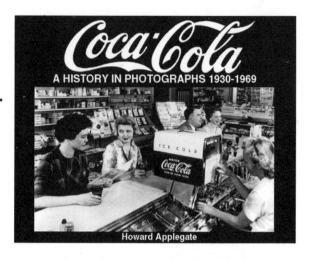

Coca-Cola
A HISTORY IN PHOTOGRAPHS 1930-1969

Howard Applegate

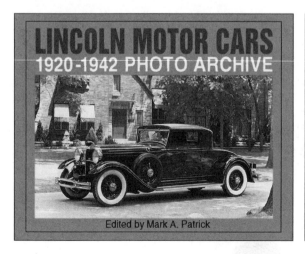

AMERICAN SERVICE STATIONS
1935-1943 PHOTO ARCHIVE

Edited by M. Kirn

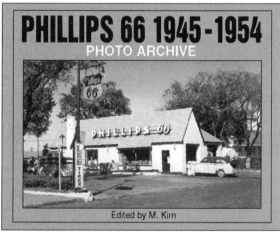

PHILLIPS 66 1945-1954
PHOTO ARCHIVE

Edited by M. Kirn

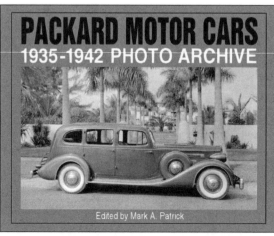

LINCOLN MOTOR CARS
1920-1942 PHOTO ARCHIVE

Edited by Mark A. Patrick

PACKARD MOTOR CARS
1935-1942 PHOTO ARCHIVE

Edited by Mark A. Patrick

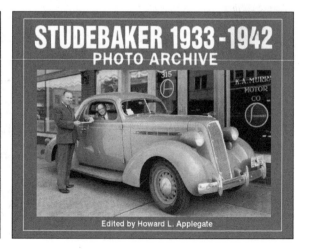

STUDEBAKER 1933-1942
PHOTO ARCHIVE

Edited by Howard L. Applegate